MW00915567

BETTING ON HORSE RACING

(No Experience Necessary)

TONY WARREN

authorHOUSE®

AuthorHouse™
1663 Liberty Drive
Bloomington, IN 47403
www.authorhouse.com
Phone: 1-800-839-8640

© 2009 Tony Warren. All rights reserved.

No part of this book may be reproduced, stored in a retrieval system, or transmitted by any means without the written permission of the author.

First published by AuthorHouse 12/7/2009

ISBN: 978-1-4490-2802-2 (e)
ISBN: 978-1-4490-2800-8 (sc)

Library of Congress Control Number: 2009911217

Printed in the United States of America
Bloomington, Indiana

This book is printed on acid-free paper.

Content is arranged as a sequence of questions that range from the simpler to the more complex issues involved in placing a bet and understanding the process of wagering on horses.

This book is intended for novice race track attendees. If you only attend the races on special racing days such as Kentucky Derby day, Preakness day or Belmont day, the book will give a greater insight into wagering on races and may perk your interest enough that you might try the races more than a few times a year.

I realize the whole process of wagering on races may seem a bit overwhelming. If you read all the information provided, I think you will have a greater appreciation of how much fun you can have from wagering on horse racing. The book will not delve into the sophisticated handicapping of races but rather focus on ways to make a wager and what types of wagers to make. The idea of this information is to allow you to make small wagers that potentially offer a nice return for that small amount of money wagered.

We will concentrate only on thoroughbred racing in our discussion. The other main type of racing in the United States is harness racing. Arabian, steeplechase and quarter horse racing are also seen in the United States but are only seen at a few smaller race tracks. The harness races are races where a driver sits in what is called a sulky and the horse pulls the driver around the track while he sits in the sulky. Some people refer to these races as chariot races. These races are a whole different game although many of the definitions used here will still apply to harness racing. The major difference between harness racing and thoroughbred racing is that in thoroughbred racing a jockey rides atop the horse and in harness racing the driver is pulled in the cart or sulky.

The big money in horse race wagering is done on thoroughbred racing and since thoroughbred racing is my passion we will concentrate on those types of races.

Each year, in the United States alone, there are thousands of races run. In those races, hundreds of thousands of horses compete. Racing throughout the world expands those numbers dramatically.

There is an old adage in horse racing that tells us "you can beat a race but you can't beat the races".

The point here is that if get into horse wagering on a more serious level, you should not bet every race you see. Be selective on the number of races you play each day. If you attempt to wager on every race presented to you, then you will lose. You should pick one or two tracks a day to wager on and then wager only on races that seem playable by our standards to be discussed later. The idea is to bet small to win large. That is easy to say, of course, and hard to do. I will try to show you how it can be done.

When we talk about wagering small amounts of money to win large amounts what I mean is the following. In a casino, when you make a five dollar bet on blackjack, and you win, the most you will win is seven dollars and fifty cents if you get blackjack. If you win without a blackjack, you win five dollars. In horse racing you can make certain wagers for as little as ten cents up to a dollar and you could win thousands. These types of wagers will be addressed in the question section later. It has happened where people have won a million dollars on a two dollar wager. This folks is not the lottery, you too can win and much of what you do to win is in your control. You can use your intelligence and not have to depend on ping pong balls to get a nice win. The most I have won on a one dollar wager was around five thousand dollars, but keep in mind I am not a high roller and my small wagers do return huge returns on many occasions.

Before we get into the nuts and bolts of wagering on races let me give you some background on how my interest in racing evolved. First of all, let me tell you up front, I am not a professional gambler. I have just retired from a sales career as a pharmaceutical sales person after thirty eight years.

Gambling has been part of my life since I was in grade school. My family would have large picnics at a lake setting where we fished, swam and played blackjack for pennies. I was around ten years old and I was totally fascinated by blackjack and since I always won I was hooked. Reflecting back on my always winning, it is now quite obvious I was being allowed to win but as a ten year old you don't know about games being fixed. I fell in love with cards and gaming.

Throughout high school I played poker with friends and won more than I lost. Just as I was about to start college I heard a harness racetrack was going to be built in my sleepy hometown of Wilkes – Barre , Pennsylvania. I didn't pay much attention to the news about the track.

I continued to play cards when I started college. Between classes, we would play cards over coffee in the cafeteria. The games were small stakes games but one could find a game anytime of the day.

I find it amusing that holdem has become such a big deal. Everyone knows the game and everyone thinks they can play it better than the pros. I never heard of holdem back in my early poker days and frankly, I wish I never heard of it now. After I've played holdem for ten minutes I am totally bored.

As my freshman year was ending, I was looking for a summer job. A friend suggested we try to get a job at the racetrack. I was eighteen and it sounded like fun. We were both hired to clean the track every morning after the previous nights races.

I started to watch the horses work out in the morning. I enjoyed the sound of the sulkies and the rhythmic breathing of the horses was calming. I started to go to the track in the evenings and watch the horses run the races. I was too young to wager as one had to be twenty one to be a player. It finally occurred to me, that even though I was too young to gain admittance to the track, I could still get in. I used my workers ID badge and if anyone asked what I was doing, I simply told them I was there to check the cleaning supplies for the following morning. I got in anytime I tried.

I found a couple of young tellers who didn't ask my age and allowed me to place some wagers. I fell in love with the sights and sounds of the track and in a sense was off and running. I spent that summer working at the track during the day and after going home for dinner I went back to watch and wager. I didn't wager much and I didn't bet every race. I just loved being there. I worked at the track the following summer as well and followed the same pattern.

Since the track was so new and so popular the local television station would show the stretch runs of the first two races every night on the news. If I couldn't get to the track I would have someone who worked there or worked with me make a couple of daily double wagers for me so I could watch those two races on television.

The track where I worked and wagered is called Pocono Downs. It is still there some forty years later. The name has recently changed and it now houses a casino and will have a large hotel built on the grounds very soon. So after many years of dwindling interest by area residents, it is now a new hot spot for the locals once again.

After graduating college, I moved to Lancaster, Pennsylvania, and all of a sudden a new thoroughbred track called Penn National was being built. It was about forty minutes from my home in Lancaster. As soon as racing started, I had to get there to see the new track and see what thoroughbred racing was all about. Penn National only raced at night except for Sunday when they raced in the early afternoon. After work, I would take the short ride to put myself under the race track lights. It was very appealing and I tried to get there about twice a month. I had a real career now and was recently married. Leaving my new wife at home at night was not a good idea. Her interest in horse racing was and still is minimal.

I had my first of two daughters while living in Lancaster. When she was four we met a couple who had a four year old son and also had some interest in the races. On Sundays we would go to Penn National for a few races with the kids and wives. We would watch and wager on about four races and then head home stopping for dinner along the way.

Talk about luck, after being in Lancaster for five years I was transferred via my job to Baltimore, Maryland. I felt like I was moving up the class ladder of racing. I went from Pocono Downs to Penn National and now on to Pimlico..

Pimlico was awesome. The first time I saw the huge complex I got the chills. The place dwarfed the other two tracks in size and structure. Pimlico is an old track located in Baltimore city. You can feel the history of the place as you approach the entrance and see in huge letters "The Home of the Preakness". The track is frankly not the most beautiful track I have frequented but I love it just the same. It is indeed, my home track. I immediately signed up to get on the mailing list for Preakness tickets and have been on the list ever since. I have seen many great races and jockeys run and ride at Pimlico. Edgar Prado, Chris Mc Carron and Kent Desormeaux all rode at Pimlico in the early stages of their careers. All three are now in the Horse Racing Hall of Fame.

In my travels, I have been to tracks in many parts of the world. I have seen some beauties and some beasts. I have been to tracks in the United States, Canada, Ireland and France. The tracks in France were by far the most beautiful. They are small brick structures that are very pleasing to the eyes. My favorite tracks in the states are Saratoga in New York and Del Mar in California. Both are awesome and you can smell the big money in the air.

Part two

When arriving at the track or if you are betting via the computer or phone the first thing you need to buy is some type of program that lists the horses and gives the official program number of the horses for each race. There are three types of programs that are available. There are two programs that are referred to as forms or racing programs and these are available at most tracks and at many convenience stores or newspaper shops in your area. The other program that is available generally only at the track is the track's own official program. All three have the basic information you need in order to make a wager. The track program will suffice for most of you at this point. These tools are always needed and it is remarkable how they are printed day in and day out without errors. Numerous local newspapers have a section on racing with analysis by experts who follow their local tracks. The folks who analyze the races are generally well informed and do pick winners quite often. I find the two New York tabloids to be the best. They do a great job on racing at the New York tracks.

We will not dissect all the information in the racing programs. You will gather enough information throughout the book without having to define every term in the racing programs. We will review a few key points about the program here to get you started.

On the inside cover of most of the programs you might buy is an explanation page of what you are looking at in the program. I urge you to look at this explanation page as it can answer some questions we will not discuss in the book. For our purposes the explanation page can tell you eight things you need to know. I will list those eight points and then elaborate on four of them that are most important right now. The points are:

1. What type of race is being run and what is the distance of the race
2. The last date your horse raced
3. What type of wagers are available for the race
4. Jockey and trainers names

5. The horses post position and official betting number
6. Where did the horse finish in its last race
7. Jockey's weight
8. A short comment on your horses last few races (got bumped, jockey fell off)

Most of these points will be discussed throughout the book but as mentioned, we will discuss four of the points in more detail at this point. The four points discussed now will also be discussed further in later questions but these four points are critical to your early success.

Date of your horses last race – I will not play a horse that has not raced in the last forty days. Some horses will win after a long layoff of over forty days but more will win who have raced in the past four to five weeks.

Where did my horse finish in its last race? – I generally like to play a horse that finished first through fourth in its last race if the race had at least eight horses in the race. I want my horse to show some recent good form of running well. Long term data suggests that a horse that ran first through fourth in its last race will win more races than those that ran fifth or worse in their last race. I would put the percentage on one of these horses winning at around thirty per cent.

What about the trackman's comments? - I like to read the comments made by people who have seen the horses' last races. I might play a horse that finished fifth or six in their last race if the comments point out something like, had a troubled trip or stumbled at the start. Look at the comments section but remember most of the other people wagering on the race will read them as well.

What type of race did my horse run in?

This question will be the most complicated so far so read slowly and read again if you need to. There are basically two types of races. There are claiming races and all others. The all others are Maiden Special Weight, allowances, handicaps' and stakes races. For our purposes we will consider claiming races and all the others as the same.

Claiming races are races when a horse is being offered for sale at the time of the race. These races have a set price for the horses in the claiming race. Those prices range from $2,500 to $100,000 with rare exceptions. A trainer who is registered in the states can claim (buy) a horse by putting in a claim prior to the race being run. When the race is over the horse is now his. The person who owned the horse during the running of the race does collect any winnings from that race but no longer owns the horse. If the claimed horse gets hurt or in some cases dies during the race the new owner still owns it and is responsible for it from that moment forward.

The other types of races are generally for the better horses or when an owner just does not want to risk losing the horse via a claim. These horses can't be claimed or bought in any race other than a claiming race.

If you look at your program and a horse you like is running for a claiming price of $10,000 and has been competitive in the recent past at this same level of competition then that horse could be considered a play.

Horses move up and down the claiming ladder. A horse may move from a race where he can be claimed for $5,000 to a race where now he is being offered for $10,000. The reverse can also be seen. A horse was running for $10,000 and is now in a race where the claim price is $5,000. Horses that have been running in non claiming races also drop down to claiming races when they are not doing well against the higher competition or the owner / trainer just feels the horse is over his head in allowance races and they drop him into the claiming ranks with the hope the horse will do better against the lesser competition.

I tend to put more value on a horse running at the same level it has been running in rather than a horse going from a non claiming event to a claiming event. This is referred to in racing as moving up or down in class. If a horse has been running for a claiming price of $10,000 and now moves to a race where he can be claimed for $25,000 I like him more than a horse going the other way. If the horse was worth $25,000 last month why is he now only worth $10,000?

This class issues and raising or lowering the level of your horse is controversial. Some serious and not so serious players love horses dropping in class. I do not. Remember, if a horse is running in high priced races and doing all right then why drop him to a lower level where he can now be claimed. Some will reason the owner/ trainer is dropping the horse from say an allowance race to a claiming race to be more competitive with their horse. A lot of issues are involved in the claiming end of the business and at this point we have discussed enough for you to have enough insight into the types of races out there to move forward. Just keep this in mind. You can't buy a mint 1955 T Bird for the price of a used cab. If a owner/trainer is offering what looks like a mint car for the price of a junker, beware.

Part Three

A friend of mine won the most money I have ever seen won on a single race. Let me back up on the friend part for a moment. His name was Stu and he and I went to the track quite often and we played poker together once a week for several years. We did not socialize outside of these two gambling interactions.

Stu made a wager called the double triple one afternoon at Pimlico. The wager has been discontinued for the most part although I saw it resurface last year at Tampa Bay Downs and this year I have not seen it again. The wager was discontinued because it lent itself to wise guys getting involved and when the tracks realized what was going on they stopped offering the wager.

The way the wager worked was one had to buy a triple ticket where you had to pick the exact order of the first three finishers of a selected race. Anyone with a correct ticket on that race took the ticket back to a teller and made a second triple selection on another selected race on the program. If no one picked the triple in both races, the money in the pool would carry over to the next racing day. Sometimes the pool carried over for several days and the pool could be several hundred thousand dollars. When the pool got to be huge, people who won the first half of the wager were selling their first half ticket to wise guys who would give them several hundred dollars for the ticket depending on the size of the jackpot. These guys would then have multiple tickets to use to make the second part of the bet and the more live tickets you had increased your chances of hitting the second triple and taking down the big money. How do the wise guys find people with live tickets? These guys are sharp and work the crowd and can spot someone with a live ticket a block away. The tracks did not like this activity so the wager has pretty much disappeared.

Back to my friend, who hit the double triple. He bought two tickets on the first race of the double triple at a cost of three dollars a ticket. It was at Pimlico .He hit on one of the two tickets on the first race of the double triple and then turned around and with that one ticket he hit the second part of the wager. With one live ticket, it is really, really difficult to do but he did it. He won $184,000.

The biggest race day of the year is, of course, Kentucky Derby day. The amount of money wagered on that day alone is often greater than the amount of money wagered at some small tracks for their entire race meet. The pools are huge and if you can find a long shot or two, you could have a great money making day.

The most I ever won on the Derby was on a win and place bet I made on a horse called Lil E Tee. I had $60.00 to both win and place on him. He paid $60.00 for each $2.00 to win on him. I can't remember how much he paid to place but that bet was a big one for me. Why the big bet from a small time bettor? I had been winning the entire day prior to the derby race and each time I would go to cash a ticket I would put some of the winnings back through the window on the derby race. I didn't even know how much I had on him until he won and I pulled the tickets from my wallet. I had watched this horse for two years and he was being ridden by my favorite jockey, Pat Day, and I knew he could win. He did.

When you are deciding on a track or tracks to wager on remember the intent is to wager small amounts to win large amounts. In order to accomplish this you need to make your wagers at tracks where the big money is being wagered. The reasoning is that in order to win large from small bets you must wager at a track that has pools of money large enough so that if you do win you are sharing in a large pool of money. You could even be the only one in the country to have a winning ticket on a race and if you are; your investment will certainly pay well.

What I mean by this is that at the larger tracks, the amount of money in a pool on a particular type wager might be $50,000. At a small track the pool on the same type of wager might be $10,000. If you happen to have the only winning ticket on a particular wager your payoff is obviously higher at the track with more money in the pool. The chances of you having the only winning ticket is slim so if you do have the only winner your share at the bigger tracks is where you want to be. If the pool is $50,000 and ten people have a winning ticket you still receive $5,000. If the pool is $10,000 and ten people have it, your share is $1,000. The pool size means a great deal.

The United Sates tracks with the largest pools are the tracks in New York, California, Kentucky with Maryland, Florida and Illinois, following in no particular order.

The wager I spend most of my time and dollars on is called the Pick 3. We will define the wager later. The average pool at the New York and California tracks is around $50,000. The Pick 3 pools at Philadelphia Park average $3,000. Of interest, the overall wagering at the tracks in Illinois ranks high but the Pick 3 pools at Arlington Park in Chicago are the smallest I see anywhere. I can't figure that out. So if a track averages $50,000 for its Pick 3 pools and another averages $3,000 guess where I will be putting my Pick 3 dollars.

The best day to wager at all tracks is Saturday. Exceptions to Saturdays are opening days at Saratoga, Keenland, Churchill Downs and Gulfstream Park. Saratoga in upstate New York has a short racing meet but the pools are generally high every day of the meet. The lightest days of racing are Monday and Tuesday. Many of the major tracks do not run on these days. Holiday racing on a Monday is the exception with big crowds and large pools.

No book on gambling would be complete without a horror story about a tough loss while gaming. I will tell you the story now so we can take a break from taking about the horses. I was visiting my sister in law in Massachusetts in the late 1970's just when state lotteries where in their infancy. Massachusetts had a game where six balls were drawn. The idea of the game was to pick the six numbers in the exact order in which they were drawn. You could make one dollar wagers on picking the exact order of the first three numbers, the first four, the first five, or all six. This was the first time I played a state lottery and thought it was fun.

It was time for the drawing, and I was ready to win. I watched the television with anticipation. The first number was drawn and I had it. The second came up and I had it. If I got the third I probably would win around $500. I got it and then got the fourth, so now I am thinking $10,000 at a minimum. I started screaming to my wife and sister in law that I had just won a lot of money and the fifth ball came out. I had it. I am now thinking $250,000. The final ball pops up and I did not have that final numbered little ping pong ball. All of a sudden, my sister in law starts crying, and I am thinking that she is so happy for us that she just burst into tears. In between sobs, she tells me I am watching the lottery drawing for Rhode Island not Massachusetts. She lived near the border of these two states and the channel I was watching was a Rhode Island channel. I had five numbers in a row but in the wrong state. My $250,000 was now zero. I went from a state of jubilation to one of downright silent sadness. Needless to say, when I checked the numbers for Massachusetts I didn't have even one in the correct order.

Before we proceed to the question and answer section; which will be the final section, we should discus tellers and the teller machines at the tracks. You can go to a teller and place your wagers or you can obtain a credit voucher from a teller machine or from a live teller. If your wagers are simple and you are comfortable you can use the machines. If you are trying a machine for the first time and are having difficulty, someone like me is always around to help a newcomer figure out what to do. If your wagers are more complicated you can ask a teller for assistance. Unless they are extremely busy they are generally more than inclined to walk you through your bet. One good use of the machines is to be able to ascertain what a particular bet will cost before you make the final decision on making a wager. Some wagers such as a superfecta can be difficult to figure out the cost of the wager. All you do is put a small voucher in the machine (a dollar or two) and make your wager and push print ticket. Because you do not have enough money on your voucher to cover the bet, the machine will tell you how much the bet costs and tell you to add money to cover the difference. You now know how much you need to invest to make a wager you were not sure about.

A word of caution is needed about both tellers and the betting machines. The tellers can get very busy at times as people can be choosing from twenty tracks to wager on within a five minute window. Most tellers are experts and honest and will get your bet punched out correctly. Before you leave the teller, check your tickets to make sure they got the right track , the right race the correct type of wager and that the amount of money you gave them is stated on your ticket. I have been given the wrong track or wrong race and once the race starts there are no refunds. Although rare, I have had tellers try to get into my pocket. The tellers who might try to pull a fast one on you are generally seasoned tellers. They can tell you are new to the track and can see you coming. Two things to watch for are what is called a slow count and the other is for the teller to not to have totally cleared their machine prior to you buying your ticket.

In the slow count, the teller is given a large denomination bill by you. Let's say a fifty. The teller will start giving you your change after you made a wager of six dollars. They will quickly give you fourteen dollars change hoping you will just walk away. All the while they will keep their other hand in their cash drawer and if you don't walk away they will pull the rest of the money up and give you the rest. Think of it as a slow or defective ATM where you are getting a withdrawal of $40 and the first twenty comes out quickly and the other $20 gets stuck for a second then finally comes out. Just be careful. The other way these sharpies can play you is leave a balance due on their machine. One simple way they do this is to make a bet for them self and leave their machine open. The next person who comes up to bet makes several wagers and is not positive how much they actually bet. The bettor may have only bet $16 but the machine shows the bettor he owes $21. An astute bettor will know what he bet but there are times when haste makes waste and we pay the teller and just walk away. The teller got a free bet on us.

When using the automated machines you must always remember to push the return balance button when you are finished using the machine. I know that seems simplistic but I have left machines with a balance on the machine and in the time it takes you to turn around and go back to the machine the balance will be gone. I have also found balances on machines and if no one is around I have kept the change so to speak. If you left a balance on a machine, don't waste your time and energy trying to find out who may have taken it. It is gone.

A final word on tellers is indicated. On very busy days such as Derby or Preakness day the tracks hire extra part time tellers who have little or no experience. If you can avoid them do so. They generally have some type of different shirt on than the regulars. They are not trying to rip you off; they just don't have the experience to keep up with the pressure of these busy days. They tend to make some mistakes. One way to avoid getting a new teller on a busy day is to buy a voucher when you arrive at the track and use it, again if you are comfortable using the machines.

Wagering via the computer or telephone is becoming more popular every day. It does hurt the race tracks in many ways. The two computer companies I have used are TVG and Express Bet. Both offer television viewing of most races each day and night including races from Europe, Australia and Japan. Both companies are first class and offer insightful information about racing and picking winners. I have to admit that on a cold December day it is easier to make some wagers at home via the computer. On the other hand, being at the track does offer interaction with friends and other bettors and is really more fun. I have had no problems in collecting winnings from either of the two mentioned television computer based companies. Another small issue with telephone wagering is that the one I use has a telephone system that will not allow me to call from a state that is not a participant in their system. The calls are blocked from land lines and cell phones. I am not sure if the other company has the same telephone issue. If you are in a non participating state when using a computer you can say you are logging in from your home state and that will work. I even tried to log from Italy and it works. It is up to you to decide which network works best for you.

I know there are other computer based companies out there but I have no experience with them so any comment would be unwarranted on my part. I stick with what I know best and HRTV(Express Bet) and TVG work very well.

A word about the integrity of the game enters some people's minds and in the past stuff has happened. It is my opinion that races at the major tracks discussed so far are never fixed. The jockeys at these large tracks make a lot of money. Six figures is not uncommon. Seven figures is also possible for a few top jockeys. The jockeys make too much money to throw races. The owners have too much money to fix races and the trainers can make enough money without the bother of trying to convince a jockey or jockeys to help them win a race. Maybe, I am being naïve, but I feel the game is on the up and up virtually all the time. On the other hand, remember the cliché, never say never.

Now let's move to some questions and answers that will help you understand how to make wagers and how to potentially win some big money for those small investments. We will also discuss many terms used around the track that will give you some insight into the language of a race track.

What types of wagers can I make?

If you want to get started and play a lot of races without spending large sums of money then wagering is as simple as 1, 2, 3. We will start with the win, place and show wagers. These wagers will not offer huge returns as will some of the wagers to be discussed later but they do offer you an opportunity to get involved and have fun without risking too much money. We will later discuss what are called the exotic wagers where huge returns can be had for minimal investments.

A win wager simply means you are betting that your horse wins the race. If your horse wins the race so do you. When betting to win all you have to do is look at the odds board at the track or on your television and you can figure out what your horse will pay if he wins. Win bets are made using two dollars as the reference point of the wager. If you bet a horse that is 2 to 1 and he wins you will receive around six dollars back for each two dollars bet to win. You will never win less than six dollars and never more than six dollars and ninety cents.

Remember the odds can change right up to the moment before the race is declared official. The reason for this possible change is that sometimes money from other tracks or computer players is still being calculated as the race is being run. It works both ways. I have had odds go up on some horses and down on others. Most players only remember when the odds go down at the last minute. The odds changes are generally small unless the horses' odds are high where I have seen changes of up to five points on an odds change. For example, a horse that may be 25 to 1 at post time may end up at 30 to 1 when the final odds are posted. When the odds are low on a horse the odds will not change very much at all.

If you make a win bet on a horse and the horse is scratched (does not race) you get your money back. There are two exceptions to horses being scratched that are worth noting. Sometimes a race will have two horses running as an entry. You will see in the official program a number 1 horse and a number 1A horse. This means if you bet on the 1 horse in a race with an entry that you actually are getting both the 1 and 1A as your horses. Occasionally you will see a 2 and a 2B and the same concept applies. If either part of the entry wins you win. The unique exception mentioned earlier happens in New York racing at the three major New York tracks of Belmont. Saratoga and Aqueduct. If you wager on a race with an entry and after the wagering has started one of the entry horses is scratched you receive a refund on any wager involving the entry. If part of the entry still races and happens to win you will only get a refund. The actual winning horse will be the horse that ran second to the entry horse that ran. By being scratched after wagering has started means that one part of the entry ran off prior to the race or was declared a non starter because he got hurt or appeared ill to the track vet. This is a strange rule that even baffles bettors that play every day. The New York tracks are the only ones that have this rule. If you wager in any other state if one of your horses in an entry is scratched you still have the other part and if he wins you win. Horses run as entry when one owner has more than one horse in a race. In the past when a trainer had two or more horses in a race they would run as an entry but that is not the case any longer.

Place Bets

A place bet means you are betting your horse will run first or second. Your horse does not have to run second for you to win money. If he wins you still win but you only receive the place money on your bet, not the win price. No odds are posted for place bets since two horses will place in each race and one can't calculate what a horse will pay to place because the price depends on how much is wagered on your horse and the other horse that places with your horse. Place bets will generally pay less than a win bet but exceptions do occur. Educated players can look at the place pool and make an educated guess on what their horse might pay to place but it is only a guess because they don't know what other horse will place along with their horse.

Show Bets

A show bet means your horse can finish first second or third and you win money. Again, it does not have to finish third for you to win. It can finish anywhere in the top three finishers and you win. Remember as in the place bets where two horses get paid you now have three horses sharing in a pool. What this means is that generally the show prices will be much lower than a win price and lower than a place price. An average show bet will return around $2.80 if the winning price on a horse is around $8.00 or in other words a horse whose win odds are 3 to 1.

As an aside, a track is obligated to pay a minimum of $2.10 for a $2.00 show bet. The only state that pays a minimum of $2.20 per $2.00 bet is Massachusetts.

What is Across the Board?

Betting across the board is an old term which simply means you are betting one horse to Win, Place and Show all on the same ticket. If your selection runs first, second or third you get some money back. If your horse wins the race you win all three of your bets. You would get money for the win part, place part and show part. If your horse runs second (places) you receive the place and show bets as a winning part of your ticket. If the horse runs third (shows) you receive only the money that the horse paid to show.

If you want to make this type of wager you tell the teller you want Race 1 at Belmont $2.00 across the board on the 2 (horse) . The bet will cost $6.00.

What is a scratched horse?

When the official program is created for the racing day each horse slated to run is listed with his official program number. If something happens to the horse or if the weather conditions change, the horse may be taken out of the race. This taking the horse out of the race is called a "scratch". If a race is scheduled to be run on the turf or grass and the race is taken off the turf course due to weather conditions you will generally see numerous scratches prior to the running of this type of race. Late scratches of horses do occur after the betting has started and refunds or consolation payoffs will result because of a late scratch. The implications of a late scratch will be discussed in more detail in the sections that discuss multiple race wagers such as a pick 3. All win, place show bets are refunded. If you have an exacta, trifecta or superfecta wager you will receive a refund on the part of your ticket that includes a scratched horse. If your ticket consists of a horse that must be part of the combination to win, you will get a full refund of that type ticket. For example, if you play an exacta of # 2 with # 4 and the either the # 2 or # 4 are scratched you get a full refund since your ticket can't possible win since only one of your horses is in the race.

If you bet on a race with a # 1 and a # 1A and one of them is scratched at any time you still have a live bet except at the major New York tracks. That New York rule on entries will be discussed under the questions on pick 3s and pick 4s

What is a Daily Double?

Back in the old days the only so called exotic wager that could be made was called the daily double. It was always a bet that was made on the first two races of the day and the object of the wager is to pick the winners of two consecutive races and in the early days of racing this again was a wager available on the first two races of the day. Today the daily double wager can be made at some tracks on every two consecutive races on the program. New York, Tampa Bay, Santa Anita and Turfway Park are four that immediately come to mind. In New York, the daily double has been and remains a very highly played wager. The pools are huge and I am not sure why it remains so popular especially in New York. Maybe the smart New York money likes the value the double offers. I like to play the double myself but again as will be discussed later I do prefer the Pick 3 wager which requires one to pick the winner of three consecutive races in a row.

The double can be played in many ways. One can pick one or more horses from each race and create a value ticket if one of your longer odds horses wins either leg of the two races. You can also take one horse in one of the two races and play every other horse in the other race so if your one horse wins you will have an automatic winner since you have all the other horses in the other leg. At many tracks you can now play a double for a dollar wager for each bet. At some tracks you must play a $2.00 double wager.

You go to the teller and say Belmont race 1, a $1.00 double of 123 with 123 and if the 1, 2 or 3 win the first race and the 1, 2 or 3 win the second race you win the double.

The double is a good wager especially if you can find a horse in each race with odds of 5 to 1 or better.

The best tracks to play a double are the New York and California circuits as the pools are always good at these venues.

What is a Bridge Jumper?

You might hear the term bridge jumper while you are at the track or listening to a race show on TV. What this means is that all of a sudden someone will notice that the amount of money in the show pool has gone from an average of $3000 at a track to anywhere from $100,000 to $300,000 on a particular race. The sudden appearance of hundreds of thousands of dollars to show on a horse catches players' eyes. Bets like this can appear at any track on any given day but is certainly not an everyday occurrence. This type of wager is usually made on a race with five or six horses in the race and one of the horses looks like an absolute standout and in the bridge jumper's eyes certainly will run as one of the top three finishers in that race. Let's say the horse has run twenty times and has finished in the top three finishers 18 of the 20 times it has run. This is the type of horse a bridge jumper will consider.

If the horse does show, the bettor will receive $2.10 for each $2.00 bet and thus get five percent on their money in less than five minutes. The average rate on a one year CD is around 3 % The one state that is the exception to paying five cents on a dollar is Massachusetts where the tracks are obligated to pay ten cents on a dollar so you would get $2.20 for every two dollars wagered compared to $2.10 in virtually all other states.

Most times the bridge jumpers are correct and their horse does come in among the top three finishers for them. On the other hand, I have seen these bets lose and when they do the prices for the other horses that do show are enormous.

About six years ago, I attended the races at Pimlico on the day before the Preakness and a bridge jumper showed up and bet several hundred thousand dollars to show on a horse running in a race called the Black Eyed Susan Stakes. There were six horses in the race. I thought this was crazy as in my opinion I did not think the horse would show at all. I bet $20.00 to show on the other five horses in the race. His horse ran fourth. I had $20.00 to show on the other three horses than did show and knew my payoffs would be very good. My recollection is that for a $2.00 show bet the other three horses paid $40.00, $60.00 and $80.00 to show. For my investment of $100.00 on show bets I got back $1800.00 in five minutes.

Many savvy players will take a chance on a wager against the bridge jumpers with the hope his horse does run worse than third. I think I have beaten the bridge jumpers five or six times in my racing life. It is fun to try with just a few dollars to show on say two or three other horses in the race. Even if the jumper is right and you have two of the horses to show you will only lose a couple of dollars.

Remember that no bet is fool proof. The bridge jumpers are called bridge jumpers for a reason. I do not think I would jump off a bridge if I lost several hundred thousand dollars on a horse but it must be downright painful to say the least.

In 2007 at the Preakness a fellow I heard about made a $100,000 show bet on Barbaro and when Barbaro broke thru the gate prior to the race the man got back in line to try to cancel the bet. When a horse breaks thru the gate prior to the start of a race it usually does not bode well for the horse or its backers. Well, the line was too long and the race started and the man was stuck with his $100,000 ticket. Barbaro ran about fifty yards and broke his leg. This guy was not a bridge jumper. He was a large bettor who knew he should cancel the bet. The fans in the betting line in front of him and the horse both cost him a lot of money.

Before moving on to the other types of wagers one can make on a race, it is probably a good time to make a few simple points on how to place a wager. If using a teller, you need to first tell them what race track you want to wager upon and then the race number of the race you are betting on. You can bet any race at any time during the day so you must tell the teller what race you want to play. Some players go to the track and bet every race at a select track and then head home and watch the races on TVG or the Express Bet channel. The next thing you must tell the teller is how much you want to bet and what type of bet you want to make. Then tell them the number or numbers of the horses you want to play. An example would be: Belmont … race 1 … $2.00 to win on number six or Belmont race 1 … $4.00 … win, place and show on number six. That bet by the way would cost $12.00. When we discuss the more exotic wagers you can make the same principles apply. Remember; always use the official race program to get the number of the horses you want to play. Some people will try to use a local newspaper to get the official betting numbers and for a beginner there are some issues with trying to do that. So buy the race track program. It will cost three or four dollars. Never use the horses name to make a bet. Use their official number and if you are betting a race with en entry in that race such as a # 1 and # 1A just say # 1. There is no need to say # 1 and # 1A. The ticket given to you will also only say # 1. It will not say # 1 and # 1A but if either one of them wins, remember you win. Now back to the questions.

What is an exacta, perfecta or exactor?

First of all, all three of the names above mean the same thing. Some tracks use different names for the same bet although exacta is the most common term used in the United States.

An exacta is a wager where you must pick in exact order the two horses to finish both first and second in a given race.

An exacta will pay more than a win wager virtually ninety nine per cent of the time. Exacta potential payoffs are generally posted on monitors throughout the tracks or you can view them on line if you are playing from your computer. It takes a bit of practice to read the potential payoffs but after viewing those for a few times you will get it. Some tracks do show them in different ways but it becomes easy to figure out after a few races.

An exacta can be played three ways. You can play a straight exacta which means you play one horse to win and another to run second. On your ticket it would appear like this Belmont Race 2 … $2.00 exacta # 1 and # 2. This bet would cost $2.00 and you will win if the finish of the race is the # 1 wins and the # 2 horse runs second. Any other finish and you do not win.

You can also play an exacta box. In a box bet you win if your horses run first or second in any order. If you play an exacta box of horses # 1 and # 2 and if those two horses run first or second in either order you will win. The bet costs double the amount of the straight exacta because you have two bets in place of one. A $2.00 exacta box of two horses will cost $4.00. Remember that at most tracks you can play an exacta box for $1.00 so the cost would be $2.00. When making an exacta box wager, simply say Belmont …race 1 $2.00 exacta box of # 1 and # 2 and pay your $4.00.

Another way to play an exacta is called a wheel or part wheel. In a wheel, you pick one horse to win the race and every other horse to run second. You tell the teller. Belmont Race 1 …$1.00 exacta … # 1 with all. If there are nine horses in the race the wager will cost $8.00. If the horse you picked to win, the # 1 horse wins you will win since you have every other horse in the race picked second.

The last way to play an exacta is a part wheel. In a part wheel you take one or two horses to win the race and take a few more to run second. In a part wheel you could take the # 1 horse to win and the # 2, 3 and 4 to run second. The wager would cost $3.00 for a dollar exacta. You could reverse this bet as well and take the # 2, 3, 4 to win and # 1 to run second and again this would cost $3.00. If you want to get a bit fancy from the beginning you take a couple of horses to win and then take those two along with three of four more to run second. The ticket would like this. Belmont …Race 1 $1.00 exacta …

1-2 with # 12345 and the cost for a $1.00 wager would be $8.00. On this ticket, if the # 1 or # 2 horse wins the race and the # 1, 2, 3, 4, or 5 horses runs second you will win. You can obviously do this in reverse order as well for another $8.00 you can take # 1,2,3,4 and 5 to win and # 1 and #2 to run second. When making a part wheel wager simply tell the teller you want Belmont Race 1 … a $1.00 exacta part wheel and say 1 and 2 with 12345. I have now left out the word number because you really do not need to say number 1 or number 2 just say the number and they will have it.

Exacta boxes can also be made using more than two horses. You can box as many horses as you think you need to win but keep in mind that every horse you add to a box costs more money. A three horse exacta box for $1.00 costs $6.00 and a four horse box will cost $12.00 for a $1.00 bet. A three horse exacta box means that you have three horses on your ticket and if any two of the three run first and second you will win. What you have would be six potential winning combinations. If you boxed horses 1, 2 and 3 you will win on any of the six combinations of 1, 2 and 3. If the race ends with any of these six combinations you win. The combinations would be 1& 2 , 2&1, 1&3,3&1,2&3,and 3&2.

As mentioned, you can box as many horses as you like but remember to view the potential payoffs if you are boxing more than three horses in a race. If you get up to thinking about a five horse box which will cost $20.00 for a $1.00 win look at the potential payoffs and if several are going to pay less than $20.00 if you win then think twice about making that wager. Most players box three horses in their exacta plays. Note of caution, when looking at exacta potential payoffs on a monitor or elsewhere remember the prices being shown are generally based on a $2.00 wager. So if you playing $1.00 exactas, remember you will only receive one half of the posted winning price

I play exactas on occasion and tend to play three horse boxes when I play. If I love two horses I will play only the two in a box and put a few more dollars on it and hope it hits. If I come up with a horse that has odds of greater than 10 to 1, I will sometimes take him to win and all the other horses to run second. This is where the gambling comes into play. If you like a horse that is 10 to 1 is it better to just bet him to win? Many times yes, but if you are trying for that big win for a small investment then taking the horse to win in an exacta and hoping another long shot runs second is worth a shot. If your 10 to 1 wins and the favorite runs second you will probably have been better served to play the 10 to 1 shot to win. The profit would probably be higher on the win bet.

What is a Quniella ?

Some tracks, not all, offer a wager called the quinella. A quinella is like an exacta in that your ticket must have the exact two finishers of a race to win. Unlike an exacta in a quinella your two horses can run in any order and you win. In other words if you play a quinella involving the # 1 and # 2 horses if they run first and second in either order you win. Remember in an exacta you must pick the exact order of finish of the first two horses. You can bet a quinilla box just like you can bet an exacta box. If you box three horses in a quinella box, the cost would be half of what it would cost to box three horses in an exacta box. An exacta box of three horses for $2.00 would cost $12.00 because you have six bets on your ticket. A quinella box of three horses for $2.00 would cost $6.00 since you only have to correctly pick the first two horses but not in exact order. The three combinations you would have would be 1/2 , 1/3 and 2/3 . Since either order of first and second is a winner, you only have three bets although you do have six ways to win..

A quinella is a fun bet but virtually on every bet it pays about half what an exacta would pay. I rarely make a quinella wager. I did play them when I started playing the horses because it looked like fun and costs less to wager than exactas.

What is a trifecta (triple) (Tri)?

Remember that an exacta is picking the correct order of finish of the first two horses in exact order. If you add a third horse to the bet it is called a trifecta or triple as it is now commonly referred to. So now you need the first three horses in exact order to win this bet. Yes, it is getting more complicated and harder to accomplish but as the difficulty increases so do the payoffs. Picking the winner of a race is sometimes hard enough but then picking the second and third place finishers in exact order makes it even more difficult.

The same principles apply to betting a triple as with an exacta wager. You can make a straight triple wager, for example, # 1 to win, # 2 to place and # 3 to show. You can also box as many horses as you like and can afford. If you make a straight triple wager as shown above the ticket would cost $1.00 since you only have one possible combination that can win. That is # 1 # 2 and # 3. If you box those three horses for a $1.00 wager your cost would be $6.00 since you now have six possible ways to win. If the # 1 # 2 or # 3 horses finish first second and third in any order you win. If you were to make a triple wager you would tell the teller you want, Belmont race 1 a $1.00 triple straight of 123. If you want a box you simply say a triple box and your ticket will show you that you have boxed three horses for a total cost of $6.00. If you get adventuresome and want to spend more money you can box four horses for a cost of $24.00. Every horse you add to a triple box starts costing a lot more money. I never go beyond a box of four horses and neither should you at this point. Most players do use triple boxes as part of their routine. If you want to hit a home run and think you know the exact order of finish of the first three horses then put that $6.00 for a box on a straight triple and hope for the best. If you do buy straight triples, buy them in increments of $1.00 rather than one single six dollar ticket. This will be discussed later in more detail.

The other way to play a triple is to use a key horse or a part wheel type wager. A Key wager involves picking one horse to win the race with three four or five horses or more to run second and third in any order. If your key horse wins and any of your other horses run second and third you win. The bet would look like this on your ticket: # 1 with 2345 You ask the teller for: Belmont, race 1 a $1.00 triple key. # 1 with 2345. In this case you are using four horses both second and third, giving you twelve combinations to win if your key horse wins the race. The cost would be $12.00 for a key with four horses to run either second or third. A Key horse wager with three horses to run second and third would cost

$6.00 and a Key horse bet with five horses to run second and third would cost $20.00 Just for fun, and you could consider this if you are way ahead on any given day, key one horse with every horse in the race to run second and third. Depending on how many horses are in the race the cost can be great. A simple trick to figure out how much a bet like this would cost is to look at how many horses are in the race and remove the highest numbered horse in the race and multiple the remaining number times the next highest number. If there are ten horses in the race, forget the # 10 and multiple the next two remaining horses. You would multiply 9 X 8 which is 72 and the bet would cost $72.00 for a $1.00 bet Another example would be a six horse race and keying a horse would cost $20.00 because removing the six would leave 5 X 4 and that equals 20 or $20.00.

The final way to play a triple is the part wheel. In a part wheel triple you can have several horses in any of the three positions needed to win the bet. Remember you do need the exact order of finish of the top three finishers. For example, you could take horses 1 and 2 to win the race with the 1 2,3,4,5. to run second and the 1,2,3,4,5,6,7 horses to run third . You could also, reverse any of the positions and for example, put the 1, 2,3,4,5 horses to run first and the 1,2 to run second and the 1.2,3,4,5,6,7 to run third. These bets become costly because you are creating so many winning combinations. If you want to try one, ask the teller what the bet would cost before you buy it. The way you would ask for a part wheel triple is : Belmont , Race 1 , $1.00 triple part wheel and then say 1,2 with 1,2,3,4,5 with 1,2,3,4,5,6,7

When triple betting was first introduced the minimum bet was $3.00 for each combination and the payoffs were huge because it was a new bet and the $3.00 tickets made for large pools. Triples are available at some tracks for $.50 a combination although the vast majority of tracks still have a $1.00 minimum bet per combination. The reduction in price of the triple has allowed more players to play for less money but the payoffs are obviously lower than in the past.

The triple is still a nice play especially if you can get the favorite off the ticket. By this, I mean the favorite has to run worse than third in a race where you play a triple. If you like a few long shots in a given race then a triple is worth a bet. If you only like the favorite or favorites in a race then I would suggest another type of wager. My recent experience has shown me that there seems to be more value in exactas than triples in today's market.

The triple is still a fun bet and I have seen tickets pay thousands of dollars for a few dollars invested. Tread carefully, and if you win the first one you play, do not fall in love with just playing triples. They are tough.

What is a Superfecta or Super ?

The superfecta has become a very popular play at most US tracks. The reason is twofold. You can make a super wager for as little as ten cents (usually a minimum of $1.00 in combinations) and secondly the supers pay off handsomely virtually all the time. As mentioned earlier, I have seen supers pay tens of thousands of dollars for a ten cent ticket. Again, the large payoffs are a result of having a difficult ticket to figure out.

In a superfecta you must pick the exact order of finish of the first four horses in a race. It is tough indeed and players use many different angles to try to hit these nice payoff tickets.

Playing a straight super ticket is a tough task when eight or nine horses are in a race. I rarely see anyone playing straight super tickets unless they are just playing it like a lottery and picking the same numbers every race. I think the best approach for a novice is to use the box technique as discussed earlier under exactas and triples or to play part wheels as discussed earlier as well. Start out playing for ten cent combinations and limit your boxes to five horses. A five horse super box costs $12.00. You can have a lot of fun if you are willing to wager this amount of money and hope for the best. Remember you will need four of the five you boxed to run first second third and fourth. Boxing more than five horses starts costing more than you want to spend at this point. A fun point is that if you do a five horse box your ticket will point out you have 120 combinations to win for that $12.00 but remember it only takes one other horse to finish in that top four and you lose. A four horse box costs $2.40 but you need all four of your horses to run in the top four positions. That is tough. It is possible but very difficult indeed.

The way I like to play supers is to turn the super into a triple. What I mean by this is that I play part wheels. Remember that to win a triple you must pick the exact order of the first three finishers in a race.

I take a horse I think will win and I key that horse on my super ticket. I then take three horses I think will run second and third and place them behind my horse that

I want to win. I then take every other horse in the race to run fourth. If my key horse wins and any of my three horses selected behind him run second and third I will have a winning ticket because I have every other horse in the race to run fourth. I will also take my key horse and put him in the second position on another ticket with the other three horses I like and then take those same three horses to run third. I will take the remainder of the horses to run fourth. If my key horse runs second to one of my other three and one of my other three run third I will have a winning ticket.

These are fun to play for increments of ten cents because you get a lot of action with the potential for large returns for your small investments.

The tickets would look like this # 1 to win and # 234 to run second and # 234 to run third and all to run fourth. If there are nine horses in a race the cost will only be a few dollars to make this wager. I will then take # 234 to win and # 1 to run second and # 234 to run third and all to run fourth.

The way you would buy this ticket would be as follows. Belmont race 1 a ten cent superfecta # 1 with 234 with 234 with all.

Once you get the hang of supers you can make all sorts of combinations that can involve numerous horses in different positions that can add excitement to every play. For example you can take three horses to win the race and three horses to run second and maybe one horse to run third with six others to run fourth. The possibilities are endless but remember that for every horse you add in any part of the super the cost of the ticket will go up.

What is a place all wager?

The only tracks I have seen that offer this wager are the tracks in California. I never play this wager but I have included a definition so you are aware of it. It is a unique bet and I have seen some good payoffs resulting from the wager.

The idea is to select a horse or horses in every race on the program and in California that is usually eight or nine races with ten races on select days. If your horse runs first or second in a race you have a live winner. Those that have the most first/second place finishers share the pool. Remember your horse can finish second and you could still be alive with your ticket. Thus the name Place All. I am not sure how large the pools are for this wager as again I do not play it. Maybe someday I will try it.

What is the Grand Slam?

This wager is only available at New York tracks. It is a fun bet that can be made for a small investment but the payoffs are generally not very high. The pools are small thus the small payoffs. I play this wager on occasion just for fun. There are some nuances in playing the grand slam but I will not spend much time on this wager since it is a play that is not worth a lot of time exploring.

The idea of the wager (this wager generally starts only on the fifth race in New York) is to select a horse to show in three consecutive races and then pick the winner of the fourth leg of the bet. If you have a horse that comes in first, second or third in the first three legs and you pick the winner of the fourth leg you win. You can add multiple horses to each leg to give yourself more options to win.

When making this wager you would tell the teller you want the fifth race at Belmont, a $1.00 grand slam and tell them you want 1 with 1 with 2 with 3 and 4. In this example you would have one horse to show in the first three races and two horses to win in the final leg. This bet would cost $2.00.

What is a Dead Heat?

A dead heat is when there is a tie for any position that involves a part of your wager. A dead heat can be important in up to the first five finishers in a race depending on what types of wagers you have made.

When a dead heat occurs in a race there are multiple payoffs in the exacta, triples, superfectas and other wagers involved in the race.

When you bet a horse to win and there is a dead heat for the Win, the payoffs will not reflect the posted odds on the odds board because those odds are posted based on the fact that only one horse will win. In a dead heat your win payoff will always be lower than the posted odds because there are now two winning horses so the pool is divided up among the two winners rather than one. If your horse won at odds of ten to one and the other horse won at odds of two to one your horse which was listed at ten to one will now pay only around three to one because of the dead heat.

What is a Pick 3?

This wager is my favorite. I find the wager offers great potential return for small amounts invested. The returns are not as high as the more difficult wagers such as superfectas, pick 4s, 5s and pick 6 wagers but I have done extremely well since this bet was introduced several years ago. The pick 4 through pick 6 wagers will be discussed later.

I generally make a wager costing $27.00 on my pick three wagers. I know this sounds high for a newcomer but this bet can sometimes end up being your only wager for three consecutive races. I will explain that in more detail in a minute.

My sense is that the average pick 3 pays around $100 for a one dollar ticket. I have seen this bet pay up to $10,000 for a dollar. The largest one I ever cashed was $3,000 for a dollar bet.

The basics of the pick 3 are to pick the winners of three consecutive races. Not easy, but certainly it can be done and there are many ways to create combinations to win the bet.

My most common way of wagering on the pick 3 is to select three horses in each of the three races. My ticket would look like this. 123 / 123 / 123. This ticket has twenty seven potential combinations to win so the ticket would cost $27.00 or a dollar a combination. The more horses you add to your ticket will increase your cost. Simply stated, you can calculate your cost by multiplying the number of horses you play in each race of the three races involved. For example, a $1.00 ticket consisting of horses 1234 / 123 / 12345 would cost 4 x 3 x 5 or

$60.00. You would have sixty potential combinations that could win for you.

Another way that many play the pick 3 is to take one horse in one race with two or three in another race and then take many or all of the horses in another race of the three races. You could do frontward, in the middle or backwards. Frontward would be to take one horse in the first race and two horses in the second race and then all the horses in the third race. Assuming there are nine horses in the third or last race of your ticket your ticket would cost $18.00. One horse times two horses times nine horses would be eighteen combinations or $18.00. The nice part of doing the pick 3 with a wheel of all the horses in the third leg is that if you have picked the first two legs or races correctly you just watch the third leg and cheer for a long shot to win to create a good pick 3 payoff.

You could, as mentioned do the bet backwards and in the first race of three take every horse in that race then take one or two horses in the second and third legs. To make a pick three wager simply tell the teller you want a one dollar pick three at whatever track you are playing and tell them the numbers of the horses for each leg. You would say 123 with 123 with 123. You could make these wagers for more than $1.00 but I will explain later why you should always make these wagers for a dollar. If you want two dollars on the wager buy two tickets for a dollar each. The reason for the one dollar wager is that there are potential tax advantages in playing for a dollar. I will explain this in detail later on.

If you are having a good day and ahead a goodly amount of money you might want to put a bit more into a pick 3 and be adventuresome and pick a horse you love in one leg of a pick 3 and then play every other horse in the other two legs to complete the ticket. If your key horse wins you will automatically win the pick 3 as you have every other horse in the other two legs of the wager. I don't suggest you take a real strong favorite as your one key horse since even if he wins your potential payoff will be greatly reduced especially if another favorite wins one of the other two legs of the three. To make a wager like the one described you tell the teller you want a $1.00 dollar pick 3 at Belmont 2 with all with all, or all with 2 with all, or all with all with 2. Remember that if there are eight horses in each of the other two races your ticket would cost $64.00. It would equate to 1 X 8 X 8 = $64.00 as you have sixty four combinations to win.

Each state racing commission has its own unique rules regarding scratched horses after you have bought your pick 3 tickets. I will elaborate somewhat, but if you buy a pick 3 ticket and a horse or horses are scratched prior to the running of any of the pick 3 races do not throw your ticket away. You may get a refund or a consolation payoff depending on which track you made your wager upon.

I will give a few examples of scratch issues with pick 3 tickets. The examples are for the states I usually wager in. In New York, if you have a horse scratched in the first race or leg of your pick 3 you will get a refund for that horse or horses scratched in that first race of the three races. If you have a horse scratched in the second or third leg of the pick 3 and you have the winners of the other two legs of the bet, you will receive a consolation payoff for having two of the three winners involved in the pick 3 wager. In Maryland, if any of your horses are scratched in any part of the pick 3 you will receive a replacement horse for your scratched horse. The replacement horse will be the post time betting favorite in the race in which your horse has been scratched. Say for example, the number 2 horse is the favorite after the race is run you have the 2 horse as your replacement horse.

In California and Florida you do not get a post time favorite as a replacement. You will receive consolation payoffs like New York.

The rules on pick 3 wagers are so difficult when scratches occur that even everyday horse players are heard asking " what happens at this track now that my horse has been scratched" ?

One thing you need to know about a pick 3 ticket in New York is that if you have a scratched horse in the first race of your pick 3 ticket you will not be able to cash that ticket to get your refund until all three races of the pick 3 are completed. Put the ticket in a safe place until later in the day and then cash it.

A word of caution is needed regarding tickets and cash. If you are seated at a table do not leave tickets or cash or even your program at the table if you leave the table. All might be gone when you return.

The best thing to do with any pick 3 tickets you are not sure about is to wait until the three races of your pick 3 are completed and take it to a teller or machine and see if it is a winner. If you use a teller just give them the ticket and they will process it and see if it is a winner. Do not tell them you are not sure. Let them run it through their computer and wait and see if a dollar amount shows up on their screen. Do not ask others about the rules (including tellers) as the vast majority of people do not know the rules for anything unusual that happens in pick 3 sequences.

One last important thing to keep in mind is that occasionally a pick 3 ticket will pay if you only have two winners out of the three races of the pick 3. This happens when you have a long shot with high odds win one of the legs of the three races and then have another horse in another leg that might have long odds as well. If the third leg of the three also produces a high odds winner there is a chance no one will have a pick 3 three ticket with a winner of all three races. The pick 3 will then pay off on what is called "two out of three". So even if you lose the first race on your pick 3 ticket and have some long shots played on the other two legs of the ticket do not discard the ticket until all three races are run to make sure you don't have a "two out of three winning ticket".

This month I helped a friend search a garbage can at Penn National for two tickets he had thrown away that were "two out of three" winners and each ticket paid over $300 . We found them and as I was the one who figured out what was happening my friend gave me a nice piece of the found money.

What is a Pick 4?

The only difference between a pick 3 and a pick 4 is quite obvious. You need to pick the winner in four consecutive races rather than three races in a row as in the pick 3. The other two not so obvious differences are that a pick 4 ticket could cost you more money if you include more than one horse in any or all four legs of the wager, The other difference is that you now have to pick four winners in a row and that becomes more difficult than picking three in a row. We will soon discuss the pick 6 and wait until you see how much that could cost and how difficult it is.

An example of a pick 4 ticket could look like this. 1,2 with 1,2,3 with 1,2.3 with 1,2,3,4. This ticket would cost $72.00 since you have 72 potential combinations to win. You could play only one or two horses in each leg of the four races and this will reduce your cost greatly. For example, your ticket could be 1 with 1, 2 with 1, 2 with 1, 2, 3 and that ticket for a dollar bet as above would cost $12.00 as you now have only 12 potential winning combinations. In the second example if the # 1 horse wins the first race of the four and the # 1 or # 2 horse wins the second race and if the # 1 or # 2 horse wins the third race and the # 1 2 or 3 win the four race of the four you would win.

At some tracks such as Turf Paradise in Arizona you can play a pick 4 for fifty cents a combination and that can be fun for your small investment.

The pick 4 payoffs are much higher than the pick 3 most of the time. They generally pay more because the degree of difficulty increases with each race you add to a consecutive race wager.

If you make a pick 4 wager and a scratch occurs in any of your races you will receive the post time favorite as a substitute for your scratched horse. Unlike the pick 3 where rules are different for each state regarding scratched horses, I know of no state or track that gives consolation pick 4 payoffs for a scratched horse. You will get the favorite as your horse. If you have a scratched horse on your ticket and are not sure if the horse that won was your substitute favorite go to the teller and ask for a printout of the race in question and the printout will show you which horse was the favorite. It will state that fact on the printout.

To make a pick 4 wager go to the teller and say Belmont race 2 , $1.00 pick 4 and then say the numbers for each race. For example, # 1 with # 1and #2 with # 1and #2 with #s 1234

What is a Pick 5?

The Pick 5 is a pick 3 or pick 4 but now another race to the mix. You now have to pick five consecutive races in a row and the degree of difficulty does increase dramatically. This wager is not available at all tracks but all the rules of the pick 3 and pick 4 apply. Regarding scratched horses, generally if you have a scratched horse you do receive the post time favorite as your replacement horse.

What is a Pick 6?

I know you already know. Yes, in a sense you have it figured out. Let's talk about this big money potential wager and some subtleties that make this a unique wager compared to the pick 3, pick 4 and pick 5.

The pick 6 wager is available at most major US tracks. The best places to play the pick 6 are at tracks located in New York and California. These tracks get the biggest play on the pick 6 and the amount of money in the pools can be very large. We will discuss why the pools can be so large after a few comments on the pick 6.

The pick 6 at the New York and California tracks require a bet of $2.00 for every combination made in the pick 6 sequences of races. In Maryland and at some smaller tracks you can play a pick 6 for a $1.00 per combination wager. For some reason I can't figure out, other tracks offer pick 6 wagering but interest is not seen by those wagering at those tracks. Check each track's rules regarding the minimum pick 6 wager before proceeding. The pick 6 at most tracks starts in the race that will be the sixth race before the end of the program for that day. In New York, the pick 6 typically starts on the fourth race and ends with the ninth race. In California it starts on the third race on weekdays and ends on the eighth race but on weekends California has nine races instead of eight races so the pick 6 would start on the fourth race. Certain tracks alter the amount of races run at their track especially on holidays and certain big racing weekends so if you are going to play a pick 6 always check the official program to see when the pick 6 starts. If you happen to arrive too late to play the pick 6 and have already made your selections throw them away and try to forget which horses you played. If you created a pick 6 and had it written down but didn't get to play it, you will never forgive yourself.

The pick 6 is unique in four ways:

- The cost is generally $2.00 for each combination you create on each ticket
- If on a given day no one picks all six consecutive winners of the six races in a row, a certain percentage of the money bet that day is paid out to those who have picked the most winners out of the six races. The fewest winners out of six I have seen are four of six.

- If on a given day someone does pick all six winners those who had five winners get a consolation payoff which is sometimes huge but most times not so huge.
- If on a given day no one picks all six winners the vast majority of the money bet or already in the pool will carry over to the next racing day and keep carrying over until someone picks all six winners on a given day.

The carryover pools can grow very fast especially in New York and California. If no one picks all six winners for two or three days the pools can reach a million dollars. People have won that much when they have the only winning ticket after a few days of no one winning the pick 6.

Keep in mind a few things about a possible pick 6 wager. Since the bet costs $2.00 for each combination on your ticket the cost of pick 6 tickets with more than one horse in each race does cost some serious money. I will give an example later.

When the pools increase in size the big time players show up and create groups or syndicates and start putting some serious money into the pick 6 tickets. They will get together three or four people and each put up a thousand or two each in an effort to have tickets with multiple combinations in order to try to take down the big prize. Four or five thousand dollars sounds like it buys a lot of combinations but when you do the math on playing pick 6 tickets you will see that even with investments like this they are not guaranteed picking all six winners.

As an example and no one would do this, Let's say four of the races have ten horses in the race and the other two have eight horses in those races. The cost of playing every possible combination available would be around a million dollars. Playing half the horses in each race would cost around $20,000. So how do we play the pick 6?

Wagers of this amount are out of the question. As an example, let's say you invest $10,000 in a pick 6 ticket and you win. What if twenty other people hit the winning ticket as well and it pays $6,000 for your winning ticket. Not a good investment. Remember you want to invest a little to make a lot and you can do that with a pick 6 but it is difficult indeed to do.

Many players try to look at all six races in the pick 6 and select two races where they feel they can select only one horse to win in those two legs of the six legs of the pick 6. When you select only one horse in a multiple race wager they are called "**singles** ". This leaves four more races to pick a winner in and many players will take two or three horses in each of those reaming four races and hope to hit the ticket. A pick 6 ticket like the one described above would look like this. Belmont race 4, $2.00 pick 6 …. # 1 - # 1 - # 1,2 - # 123, - # 1,2 -, # 1,2. The ticket would cost $48.00. You have twenty four combinations to win and each combination costs $2.00. You can see how costly a pick 6 can become especially if you start adding a horse or two to certain races of the six races of the sequence.

I have hit two pick 6 tickets. The times I have hit them were on days when numerous others hit it as well and my payoffs were around $1000. Keep in mind that my investments in the pick 6 are generally around $24.00 so my return on my two tickets was still good. I do not play the pick 6 unless the carryover pool is over $200,000 and then the most I invest in the bet is $24.00.

If you want to try for a life changing score then the pick 6 may be your way to go.

What is Dead Money?

Dead money is money being held by the track when a certain bet is not won and the money is carried over to the next racing day to be included in the pool for that day. Dead money occurs when for example no one picks a winner in the pick 6 or at Monmouth Park when no one picks the late pick 4.

At virtually all tracks in the states when a pick 6 is available and no one picks all six winners on a given day the vast majority of the money bet on that pick 6 is carried over to the next racing day. Those that hit the most winners of the six races get a payout but the big money moves on to the next day. The dead money is that money carried over to the next pick 6 that begins at the track where it was not hit on that day.

Why is it dead money? It is so called because there are no tickets alive or associated with this carry over money. The dead money is added to the amount of money wagered the next day on the pick 6. If there is not a carryover day and the amount of money bet in the pick 6 pool is $10,000 then that entire $10,000 has tickets associated with it. Each two dollars has a combination that might win. The carry over money has no tickets associated with that money. The money is added into the pool but since it has no tickets associated with it … it is dead money.

The simple thing to remember is that the dead money has no chance of winning by itself. Only live money can win the pick 6 and if your live money ticket hits the pick 6 and you have the only ticket you get the money bet that day along with the dead money carried over from yesterday. The only exception to a carryover on a pick 6 occurs on the last day of a racing meet. When a meet is ending and a pick 6 is being played on that closing day all of the money in the pool is returned to those having the most winners on their pick 6 ticket. On a closing day one could only have four or five winners on their ticket and take down the whole pool since it must be distributed on a closing day.

What is the track take out?

The take out is the amount of money each track takes out of all the money wagered on each race. This is the tracks way of staying in business. The percentage taken out of a race varies from state to state but the percentage take outs are most times very close in terms of percentage.

Generally the win, place and show bets have the smallest take out by the tracks. The exotic wagers such as exactas pick threes and superfectas have a higher percentage take out. For example on pick three and pick 4 wagers the takeout averages twenty five per cent across the U.S.

Remember you are not playing against the house as you do in a casino. Even though the track takes its cut from every wager you are still playing to win the money bet by others who wagered on your race after the track has taken its percentage. Unlike a casino, the track returns all the money bet on every race to the players after it has taken its cut of the money pools.

The tracks with the lowest percentage take out on the win; place and show wagers are New York and California. The take out on these bets is generally around fifteen percent. The exotic wagers take outs are generally the same across the country at twenty five percent. Occasionally a track will offer certain exotic wagers with a lower percentage takeout and if you place wagers at a track offering lower takeouts take advantage of the situation as it means more money will be coming back to the players.

What is simulcasting ?

Simulcasting is having numerous tracks showing its races at your home track, at an off track betting parlor or at home on your television. You can wager on races from around the world virtually all day and night. The big advantage of simulcasting is that all the money wagered on a given race is now pooled together so the pools of money are much larger than before simulcasting became the main stay it has now become. Prior to simulcasting, if you attended the races at Pimlico and bet those races you were playing against only those wagering at Pimlico. The pools of money were much smaller because you did not have any money coming in from around the world that would increase the pool of money on a given race.

How do I know what types of wagers are available for a given race or a given set of races?

The best place to find out what types of wagers are available for a given race is in the official track program. The two main racing forms now available also list what wagers are available at the top of the information about each race. Up until recently this was not being done and it caused confusion if you bought one of these papers at a convenience store and did not have an official track program for a specific day. If you were playing at home via the phone or computer it was hard sometimes to know what types of wagers were available on a given race.

The programs will tell you if a daily double, pick three or superfecta is available for the race you are looking at.

Some tracks now have multiple daily doubles starting on every race and many now have pick 3 wagering on every set of three races. Some have superfectas on every race and others like the New York tracks have them only on select races.

Virtually all tracks have win, place and show wagering on all races unless a race has less than five horses running. In that case many tracks will not offer show wagers on a race with only four horses competing. The vast majority of races offer exacta and trifecta wagering on all their races. The exception would be that a trifecta might not be available if only four or five horses are in a race. That is the case at the New York tracks. Some tracks do have rules on superfecta wagering and require that at least seven horses are in a race to offer superfecta wagering. That is the case at the California tracks.

What do everyday players use as tools that we have not mentioned?

They use numerous angles that they have picked up from experience and many use what are called speed figures ,or the so called Sheets, which give each horse a rating based on speed. They are not foolproof by any means and too complicated for our purposes at this point.

Some use the class of a horse as a key and others use breeding as part of their equation.

These tools are part of handicapping but at this point in your playing the game you need not concern yourself about these aspects of the game. If you get to the point where you are betting the races four times a week you could start weaving in some of the above tools as part of your betting plan.

What about betting systems?

I know of none that have ever proven to work. Many players use concepts and ideas they have found helpful over the years but no system has ever shown it will work over the long haul.

The only system I have tried and it can show a small profit on many days is to wait for a race where only one horse has been bet down to odds of 5/2 or less and then play that horse to place. The thing about this wager is that you might have to wait all day to find the race where only one horse is at 5/2 or less and then your horse will probably pay less than $3.00 to place. If you have the patience to make only this type of wager you will not win a lot of money but your wagers like this will cash at a high percentage.

What can I learn from watching the odds board on a particular race?

There are two keys I look for when watching the odds board that help me make a decision on which horse or horses could be part of my bets.

The first thing I look at is the first change of the odds from the morning line posting of the odds on the odds board. The track odds maker will post the odds he feels are going to reflect the betting on each race and these odds are posted immediately after the previous race has run and will remain for all to see until the money starts being bet and the odds change based on how much money is bet to win on each horse.

My experience has been that the early money bet on a race is an important indicator of where the smart money is going. Many will argue that late money or money wagered just prior to the race is more important. I totally disagree. If a horse is listed in the program or odds board at 2/1 and if the first change of odds shows this horse at 10/1 be weary of playing the horse. Many times a horse like this will have the odds fall as the race gets closer to running but in my experience more of these will lose than will win. Conversely, if a horse has morning line odds of 10/1 and at the first change of odds opens at 5/1 give the horse a second look.

The other key thing I look at on the odds board is the show pool or the amount of money bet to show on each horse in a race. With five minutes left to post time if I see a horse with more money to show on him compared to the current favorite in the win betting pool I will use that horse in my wagers in some way. Put another way, if the win odds on horse #1 are 2/1 and the #3 horse has odds of 4/1 but has more money bet to show on him then consider the 3 horse in some way. This key does not happen often but has proved a key for me in making some easy money. I think what happens when this show money shows up is that people associated with the horse think the horse will run well today and since it is not the favorite they can get a quick easy return on betting him to show. Also by betting their horse to show they can still bet him in other type wagers and not give away the fact that in reality he is more of a favorite than the betting public realizes.

What is a horse for a course?

This phrase is used when a horse runs well at a particular race track. If you look at your program you will see an area that shows how often a horse has run at this track and how well the horse has run there. If a horse has run twenty times at various tracks and never won other than at the track where he is running now take a close look at this horse. There are other reasons why the horse may run best at this track but regardless of what they might be, you could consider this horse as a major contender today because he just likes this track for whatever reason. He may not ever win at one of the New York tracks but when he returns to Maryland or Pennsylvania he can win.

What about jockeys? Where do they fit into the discussion?

Just as in any sport or competition some people are just better at their profession than others. They might be bigger, stronger and smarter than the others and that gives them an edge. The jockeys are certainly not bigger than most but some are stronger and smarter than the others and some just have an innate ability to ride race horses. The other attribute a jockey must have is a lack of fear. The good ones will slip their horse through the narrowest of openings and not even wince. One wrong move while going forty miles an hour on a horse can mean a bad accident or even death. Some jockeys have all the tools, a knack for riding and the courage that many of us might not possess.

Some jockeys win more than others. The top jockeys at any given race course will win around twenty per cent of their races. The other top ten jockeys at the same course will win between ten to fifteen per cent of their races and the bottom rung jockeys will win under ten per cent.

So what does that mean? When a jockey starts winning at a high percentage he starts being asked to ride numerous horses for numerous trainers. This type of jockey and his agent get to pick form more horses than the other jockeys and thus get to pick what they perceive as the best horse in a given race. An owner or trainer with a good horse (one they expect to do well) will generally ask the jockeys with the highest win percentage to ride their horse. If you get a jockey who is winning at a twenty per cent rate why not take him rather than one who is winning at a rate of five per cent.

This does not mean that a six per cent winning rider can't win as they obviously do and when they win the payoffs are generally higher than when you bet on a leading jockey at any track. Remember that the twenty per cent winning jockcy is still losing at an eighty per cent rate. So he is losing eight of ten races he rides in.

If you like a horse because of all the other reasons discussed or those that will be discussed than play the horse. Most of the jockeys at the major tracks can ride well and all can win on any given race.

Some players look for jockey switches. A horse was ridden by a five per cent jockey and is now being ridden by a twenty per cent jockey. Some win and most do not. Sometimes the jockey is doing someone a favor by riding this type of horse or he is looking to get connected to a particular owner or trainer for future services.

So what if I had a horse that has run twenty times and never lost? If I put the top jockeys in the country on him he would probably keep winning. If I put the lower percentage jockeys on him who ride in New York or California he would probably still win. On the other hand if I had a horse that raced thirty times and never won I could probably put the top rider in the world on him and he still might not win.

The jockey is indeed important and yes you want a good one riding your horse. But again, even the best do lose a whole lot more than they win.

What is an apprentice jockey?

Just as the name implies, they are apprentices in the business of riding horses and will try to become journeymen jockeys.

The advantage of an apprentice jockey is that during the first part of his apprenticeship the amount of weight he carries on his horses is less than the other non apprentice jockeys in a race. The difference in weight is between ten and fifteen pounds. After a certain time frame or after he has won a certain amount of races the weight is adjusted upward and then adjusted again after a year and he will still have a five pound advantage over the other jockeys.

Jockeys vary in weight just like all of us but their average weight is around one hundred five pounds. If a jockey weighs one hundred five pounds and his mount is designated to carry one hundred fifteen pounds then ten pounds of weights are added to his saddle cloth to make up the difference in assigned weight. If an apprentice is assigned to ride a horse and carry one hundred fifteen pounds and he gets a ten pound allowance for his apprenticeship then no weight would be added to the saddle for that horse to carry.

Does the weight advantage help the apprentice?

Many players look at the weight advantage as a help since the horse may be carrying less weight than others in the race. I discount the weight advantage until I see an apprentice start winning on a regular basis. As discussed prior, he is a jockey like all the rest and will win his fair share but lose more than he wins. The other downside to a hot apprentice is that when he starts winning or looks like the real deal the prices on his winning payoffs will drop sharply. Everyday players will jump on board thinking they have a good thing. Overall, I do think a good apprentice does have an edge. I have seen top apprentice jockeys lose their weight advantage and never get back to the winning percentages they showed with the weight advantage.

Keep in mind that these young riders are still learning and many will ride only as an apprentice and never be seen again. The other side of that coin is that all the top riders did start as an apprentice and made it and are still in the saddle some twenty years later.

What is OTB?

OTB is off track betting. As the name implies it is a place where you can wager on horses away from a race track. These sites could be on a street corner in Manhattan, a building in central Pennsylvania, a restaurant or at a casino anywhere in the states.

The wagering rules and regulations are the same as the state regulations for the state in which the race you are betting at the moment. The payoffs are exactly the same as you would receive had you been at the track where the race was run. The only exception I know of where a difference between track payoffs and OTB payoffs occurs is at the OTB centers in New York. If a horse pays $10.00 at the track the New York OTB will pay between $9.60 and $9.80. I am not positive on the percentage reduction paid by the OTB but I do see differences in the pay outs. At all other off track sites where I have wagered I received the payoff posted by the track. I guess you are paying for the high rent in cities, such as New York.

OTB sites do offer accessibility for many who do not have easy access to attend the races at a track. They do offer free admission and many offer free parking so you can save a few dollars if this is your fancy,

Is there any advantage to the post position (starting point) for a horse?

If you buy a racing form or a racing program you will find charts for many tracks that show the winning post positions for that track for the current meet. The breakdown is by distance of the races that have run. The chart will usually show winning post positions for races run under one mile and for races run one mile and longer.

What I have found, is that, inside post positions produce the most winners on a percentage basis. By inside post positions I mean horses staring in the number one thru three positions or nearest the rail and outward. I have not looked at all the data for every track but I have confirmed with various sites that the # 2 horse does win more races than any other post position. I have followed this data at the New York tracks for several years and the # 1 position has a slight advantage over the # 2 position. The winning percentages for the # 1 and # 2 in New York are both around 13%. Overall the # 1 horse will finish first, second or third more than any other post positioned horse. This holds true at virtually all thoroughbred tracks. It does not hold true for quarter horse racing, so if you decide to try to wager on quarter horse racing keep this in mind.

If you are making exotic wagers such as trifectas or superfectas remember to think about including horses that have inside post positions. If your choice for a horse to run first, second , third or fourth comes down to the # 1 horse or the # 8 horse consider the inside post positions first.

The post position advantage can change quickly on a given day or week at any track due to track conditions or a change in track surfaces. This is called a track bias which we will discuss in the next question.

Betting on horses # 1 and # 2 only would be a mistake but if you like the # 1 horse and the # 8 horse equally, lean toward the # 1.

Even though the inside post positions win the most races they still lose 85 % of the time so just playing the inside horses is a losing proposition. You must factor in all the available information to make a decision where to place your money. This would include the horse, the jockey, the trainer and the odds of your horse.

The simple reason the # 1 horse runs in the money more than all the others is that the horse starting on the rail sometimes can save ground on turns and does not have to run as far as a horse starting from an outside post position.

What you will learn as you watch enough races is that if the # 1 horse does not have early speed at the start of races he may lose the rail advantage because he now has to circle around other horses with greater early speed. When this occurs he loses his rail advantage.

The bottom line on post position should be to always think inside if you like two horses in the same race. Nothing in racing is a sure thing so do not just start playing the # 1 horse in every race or you will soon discover that you will lose.

What is a track bias?

A track bias is an occurrence when horses at a track start winning and keep winning from various post positions on a recurring basis. Horses running from the inside post, outside post or in the middle posts may all of sudden start winning all the races.

The reasons are not always clear as to why this occurs. It could be weather related or the track was prepared differently today or some new material was added to the track surface. Astute players will notice that no horses running out of the # 1 through # 3 posts are winning any races . You will hear the comment that the rail is dead meaning horses starting on the inside are not winning. In contrast, the horses starting in # 7 through # 9 are winning at a high percentage. Noticing a bias for horses staring in the middle of the track is the most difficult to notice.

When an astute player thinks they have found a bias they will go with it until it seems to have disappeared. The track officials may also see the bias and they will attempt to make adjustments to the track surface to make the races less biased.

The weather can affect any track and a hard dry track with an inside bias may change overnight due to rain or snow. If you think you have found a bias go with it until you are convinced it no longer exists.

Many tracks are installing synthetic surfaces. These new surfaces are made of various materials rather than the sand and dirt of the traditional courses. They are being installed because they drain better than dirt and because many feel these new surfaces make it easier on the horses well being.

Several tracks have gone to the synthetic surfaces and it is too early to say with certainty that a bias will occur on these surfaces. Keep watching and see if you pick up any bias on these new surfaces.

Another type of bias I have seen occurs only at Aqueduct in New York during winter racing. Aqueduct has two courses at the same facility. During the winter season, they race on what is called the Inner Track. The bias I have seen is that horses that have the best early speed win a high percentage of the races on this course. It seems clear that horses that try to come from behind have a very hard time winning. If a horse is running further back than first, second or third after a quarter mile of the race has elapsed they do not win very often.

Before you think I have given you a secret about Aqueduct. Keep in mind that all the jockeys know what we have discussed as do most of the astute horseplayers who play the Aqueduct races. I have told you about the bias so if you look at a program and a horse running at Aqueduct on the inner track always wins from coming from behind (a closer) keep in mind the early speed bias at this track.

If you are not yet comfortable with ascertaining information found in the racing programs a good idea would be to purchase one or both of the New York tabloids as the racing reporters usually have some helpful comments on racing in New York

What is a Maiden and how do you play Maiden races?

A maiden race horse is a horse that has never officially won a race. Maidens usually run in races with other maidens. Occasionally, a maiden will run against horses that have won races but my experience has been that they will not win against other winners.

Many maiden races often have multiple horses in the race that have never raced before. This is their first race ever. Most astute players do not wager on races like the one mentioned above. Many do not play maiden races at all. With no history to look at other than perhaps a workout, these races are most difficult to figure out.

If a maiden race has horses in it that have run a couple of races then a couple of concepts can be applied. If a maiden has run ten races and has never won I will not play that horse. If he has not won after ten tries he may never win. A second idea is that if a horse has run twice and has appeared to run competitively (maybe a second and a fifth place finish) I will give that horse a strong look. Some do well in their third start. Bottom line, maiden races are tough so tread carefully.

What about races run on the turf (grass)?

Turf races are races run on grass rather than run on dirt or synthetic surfaces. Most tracks have two courses available for racing. They have their dirt or synthetic track and they have their turf course.

I tend not to play turf races as I find them a totally different game and I have never had any luck playing them on the turf. As mentioned earlier, I tend not to play a horse that has not run in the past thirty days or so. In turf races I see horses win that have not raced in over a year.

If you want to try them my only advice is to look at the program and see how many times the horse has run on the turf and what type of record it has on the turf. If they have run on it before and seem to run well then perhaps give them a play. This information can be found on the right upper corner of the racing forms and programs.

How long are most races?

There are five common distances run in the States. They are five, six and seven furlongs and one mile and one mile and sixteenth races. Other distances are seen on occasion but these are the most common. A furlong is how races are gauged in term of distance. A furlong is one eighth of a mile. So eight furlongs would be a mile.

Races run at five or six furlongs are generally referred to as sprints. Races run at seven furlongs are not as common and fit between a sprint and a route. A race at a mile or longer is referred to as a route race.

What about trainers?

Trainers at the major tracks like New York and California are all very capable or they would not be able to afford being at high end tracks. Some obviously win more than others and their winning percentages are listed in your racing programs. There are no secrets about which trainer is saddling the most winners.

The top winning percentage trainers are looked at closely when their horses are entered in a race. They deserve the attention just as the top jockeys deserve our attention. Trainers like jockeys lose more races than they win.

Look at a trainers winning percentage and if everything else about a horse fits for you then strongly consider that horse as a play. My experience has been that high percentage winning trainers do get over bet even if their horse looks like it has no chance to win. If you find a case like that look to beat them in order to get a good payoff for yourself.

What about betting on favorites?

Favorites win 33% of all races run year in and year out in the U.S. There is nothing wrong with playing a favorite as they do win one of every three races they run in. They also lose 67% of the races they run in. Betting every favorite in every race is a losing proposition. If you play nine races at a given track the odds tell us you will win three of the nine races you played. If the three winners pay an average profit of $3.00 each, you will collect nine dollars worth of profit for your $2.00 bet to win on these three favorites. On the other six $2.00 bets you made you will lose so your loss for the day would be $12.00.

If you want to try this and play all the favorites to win you will on average cash three of nine races played and can have a nice day at the track for a loss of a few dollars. If you get lucky and get five favorites to win you will make a small profit and have some money for coffee and donuts the next day,

What about favorites to place and show?

The percentage of favorites that run first, second or third in a given race is about fifty percent. Remember that the payoffs on favorites to place and show are generally small. Most times you are talking about a dollar or two profits on place bets and a forty to sixty cent profit on show bets. You would need to cash tickets on at least six of the nine races played to show a profit.

What about playing favorites in exotic wagers such as a pick 3, pick 4, pick 6, trifecta or superfecta?

Since any multiple race wagers such as pick 3 4 or 6 (already defined) involve playing at least three races in a row it makes sense to include some favorites on your multiple race tickets. The more races involved in your sequence the better to include some favorites. On a pick 3 ticket you might include a favorite or two on two races of the three and look for a long shot or two on the third race of the sequence. The same principles should apply to pick 4 tickets.

On a pick 6 ticket it make sense to use some favorites as part of the six picks. Usually one or two favorites will win one or two of the six races. If you can create a ticket where no favorite wins and you have all six winners you will win a huge amount of money on that type ticket.

On trifecta tickets I have found that having a favorite on your ticket makes sense but if the favorite is the winner on your trifecta ticket the amount of your payoff will go down greatly. If you have the favorite to win and get two long shots to run second and third you may get some value on your ticket. If you can create a trifecta ticket where the favorite runs second or third your values will definitely increase.

On superfecta tickets having the favorite on your ticket is sometimes all right, even if the favorite wins the race. Picking the three other horses to finish behind the favorite is still difficult and I have seen superfectas pay handsomely even when the favorite wins the race. If you can create a superfecta ticket where the favorite finished third or fourth the value can sometimes soar.

When playing superfectas it is not necessary to keep a favorite off your ticket but again try to use him in more positions on your ticket than only the win position. One way to use the favorite in more than one position is to box the wager (discussed under the superfecta question) and you will have the favorite on all four needed winning positions on your ticket.

Superfectas are a fun bet but keep in mind that they are a difficult wager to win. Bet them small and have some fun with them. I have won thousands for bets as small as a dollar.

What about betting more than one horse to win a race?

Playing more than one horse to win is sometimes tried when you like two horses whose odds are greater than 10 to 1. I would not do it if one horse I liked was 2 to 1and another 10 to 1. It does not seem like a wise play. What I might do is to create an exacta ticket and box these two horses I think will win and then bet the longer priced odds horse to win.

The other time I have bet more than one horse in a race is when I am in the final race of a pick 3 or pick 4 and I have the first two or three winners already in. If my potential payoffs on the final legs of my pick 3 or pick 4 were going to pay over a $1000 I might take another horse or two and bet them to win if I do not have them on my pick 3 or pick 4 ticket. I would only do this if the odds a horse I thought could beat me are 10 to 1 or higher. If I do this I might have four or five horses in the race to win and each will still give me a profit. Some of my friends tell me not to do this and to stick with my original tickets only and not to hedge my bets.

What is a steeplechase?

A steeplechase is a race where horses are required to jump fences as part of the race. A number of fences are set at various points over a grass course and the horses are to jump every fence in the race in order to try to win the race.

Many times jockeys fall off their mounts as it is most difficult for the horse and jockeys to make all the fences in perfect order.

In Europe these races are more common than in the States. In the States, Saratoga runs some of these races each year. I have seen other tracks run a few here and there but they are not a common event. They are fun to watch but I do not bet on them. One interesting thing about these races is that no starting gate is used to start the race. The horses line up at a starting point and just start running.

What is Lasix?

Lasix is a drug that is classified as a diuretic. It basically helps reduce fluid in the body of both humans and horses. It helps reduce fluid in the lungs and helps the horse breathe better.

If you look at your program, you will see an L listed next to the horses name. This indicates the horse is running on Lasix. If it is the horses first time running on Lasix the L will have # 1 next to it.

When Lasix first started to be used on race horses you would hear players talking about it and many had theories that a horse on Lasix for the first time would perform well. Today, I rarely hear anyone mention Lasix. I don't see any advantage to playing a horse on or off Lasix.

What is a parlay?

A parlay is a bet that you make involving multiple races. You can create a win, place or show parlay or a combination of any of the three.

If for example, you want to do a win parlay you would bet a certain amount to win on a horse and if your horse won you would then take the entire amount of your winnings and place that amount on another horse to win. Let's say you bet $2.00 to win on a horse and the horse wins. You collect $20.00 for your win. You now take that entire $20.00 and bet it on another horse to win. If that horse wins you have completed a two race parlay and for your original $2.00 bet you have now profited $200.00 if your second winner paid $20.00 to win. If you have the nerve you could now put the entire $200.00 on the next race and create a three race parlay or you can stop and start another two race parlay for a few dollars. You can do the same type parlay in a place or show bet but your returns will be much lower.

What is an inquiry on a race?

Each track has what are called stewards (judges) who are placed at locations around the track to view each race to make sure nothing has happened during the race that affected the outcome of the race. If they think they saw some activity during the race which could have affected the outcome they post what is called the Inquiry Sign. The sign will be a blinking light that says Inquiry.

The main reason an inquiry could be posted is that a rider impeded another horse during the race or bumped another horse causing that horse no chance of winning. Incidental bumping is generally left alone. Bumping another horse or swerving into the path of another horse is many times enough reason for the stewards to disqualify a horse from wherever it finished. This can be any finishing position even the winner. Another type of interference occurs when a jockey hits another horse or rider with his whip or sometimes with his hands. This does occur and the horse will be disqualified and placed behind the horse he hit. Another type of incident that can trigger an inquiry is when there is a starting gate malfunction and a horse or horses do not get a fair start out of the gate. The people that help with the horses are called assistant starters and occasionally one of them will be helping hold a horse's head straight and the gates will open and the horse is being held by one of the starters. These gate malfunction or assistant starter issues are looked at under the inquiry sign and sometimes a horse impacted by these events will be considered a non starter and you will get a refund. You will also see a horse just stand in the gate after it opens and this will be looked at but if the gate opened fairly no refunds will be granted.

There are a few other unusual things that can happen but do not happen enough to discuss. Do not throw your tickets away until the inquiry sign is taken down and the race is declared official.

Only the track stewards can post the inquiry sign. A jockey or trainer or the owner of the track can't call for an inquiry.

Who are the stewards?

The stewards are officials appointed by the state to oversee racing and to make decisions about anything controversial that occurs during the running of a race. They are generally people who have been involved in horse racing for a long time. Many are former jockeys.

What is an objection?

An objection or claim of foul happens when a jockey or trainer makes a claim that his horse was interfered with by another horse or jockey. The objection involves only the jockey and his horse. A jockey or trainer can't file an objection based on issues which are governed by the stewards as discussed above. When an objection is made it is made immediately after the race is run but not yet official. The stewards will review the objection and make changes based on what they see during a rerun of the race.

If your horse has won a race, the worst thing you want to see is an inquiry and an objection at the same time. An inquiry is bad enough but an objection against your winner as well is many times not a good sign.

I have seen decisions made by stewards that I have disagreed with but for the most part they are fair and I feel impartial in their decisions. Others would disagree.

If you want to have a little fun go to a TV monitor during a review of the race and the discussions around the TV can get pretty animated as those who want a horse to remain as is and those who want a change or disqualification. Some will even make wagers among themselves about the outcome of an inquiry or objection. I think the two worst moments in terms of anxiety in racing are the photo finish and an inquiry sign.

What are layoffs or coming off the shelf?

As mentioned earlier, I do not wager on a horse that has not raced within the last forty days and most times I prefer they have run within the last thirty days.

Horses do have rest periods and the rest period is called a layoff. You will hear the term … coming off the shelf as well. You will also hear the terms second or third time back. This means the horse is now racing for the second or third time after being given a rest of over a month or more.

Very few horses are sound enough or form full enough to keep racing month after month without a layoff or rest.

My best plays are on horses coming back the third time off a layoff. I think the third time back is a key.

What about tip sheets?

Tip sheets are sold at virtually all tracks. They cost a dollar or two and I never buy them. If early on you need some help in picking some winners try the New York tabloids where that analyze New York races and some races in New Jersey and California as well. Sometimes they are very insightful.

Another thing to avoid is listening to someone at the track who walks up to you and gives you a horse that can't lose. These are called touts and if the horse they give you wins they will be back for a token of appreciation. Ignore them.

If someone you know is connected to a horse either by ownership or trainer they will most times tell you their horse has a good chance to win. What else would they say. Take it with a grain of salt. If the horse does not fit the ideas we have discussed save your money and if their horse wins offer your congrats and tell them you had a few dollars to win on their horse. It will make them feel good.

What types of horses run the Triple Crown Races?

The horses that run in these major events are all three year old horses. All thoroughbreds in the US have the same racetrack birthday no matter when they are actually born. That day is January 1. A one year old horse born on March 1, will become a two year old on January 1 of the following year. Most breeders like to have their new horses born as close to January as possible so they have a full year of life before they start racing at age two. No one year olds race. Many start racing at two and most by three years of age.

The horses that run in the Triple Crown races are generally royally bred and many were sold at age one for millions of dollars. Many of the horses that run in these big races have raced at age two, but not all.

What about wagering on the Triple Crown races?

They are indeed fun to play and some big payoffs have come from the big races. I find races of this magnitude difficult to play. The Derby has had twenty horses in the field the last few years and finding a winner out of twenty top race horses is most difficult. In the derby you have the top horses, the top trainers and the top jockeys all competing in one race where one wrong step by any of the twenty contenders can change the whole race. Last year in the 2008 derby the favorite won the race and the superfecta paid $29,000 for a dollar wager.

I do play the race and have had some good winners including two winners that paid over a hundred dollars to win for a $2.00 win bet.

The Preakness and the Belmont stakes tend to be more playable since the average size of the fields are around ten horses.

The Triple Crown races are fun and create interest for many hundreds of thousands of people every year. Make some small wagers and enjoy the extravaganza of big time racing.

What is a chalk player?

A chalk player is a bettor that generally only bets on the favorite in any given race. The betting favorite in a race is called the chalk. The reason why the favorite is called the chalk is that bookmakers back in the day would use blackboards to keep track of the odds on a race and the favorites odds changed the most during the wagering so more chalk was applied to his area on the chalkboard and more fell on the floor under his name and number.

How much does it cost to buy (claim) a race horse?

At the smaller tracks in the states you can claim a horse for $2500. Horses of this caliber will never see the bright lights of racing in New York or Los Angeles.

The acquisition price of the horse is only a small part of the expense of getting involved as an owner. The daily fee one has to pay a trainer is around $60.00 a day not counting vet bills and transportation costs. Big time trainers at the larger tracks can command $125.00 a day to train your horse. Not counting the vet bills the cost for a year of training will cost around $20,000. If your horse doesn't win his fair share of races you will spend a lot of money with your horse. Years ago, the IRS allowed tax deductions for certain race horse losses. These deductions have been eliminated and thus have eliminated many investors with little capitol to invest in a racehorse.

What about the saying ....playing with their money?

I hear people at all gambling venues saying ... I am playing with their money now. What they are saying is that they are winning and now playing with house money rather than their own money. Get that idea out of your mind. If you are winning, the money is now yours and does not belong to the house. Just because you are winning do not get carried away thinking you are betting for free. The tide can turn in a minute so if you are winning do not get caught up thinking you are invincible and do not start wagering blindly.

What is a signer?

A signer at the track is a winning ticket where you must sign an IRS form showing the amount of money you have won, if that amount of money won, fits certain IRS parameters.

The rules are not all that difficult but it does take some time to figure them out. There are also some ways to avoid signing for a large win and I will explain.

The rules on signing for a ticket are twofold:

1. The ticket must be valued at over $600.00
2. The ticket must be valued at least three hundred times the amount of your wager.

The winning ticket can be any one dollar winning ticket that pays over $600.00 for that $1.00 bet. The ticket you have may have cost $10.00 but the winning portion of that ticket may have cost only $1.00 so you must sign.

A winning ticket, where you have bet $2.00 on that winning combination and the payoff is over three hundred to one, is also a signer. For example, you played a daily double for $2.00 and the ticket will pay $700.00. Since you are getting more than three hundred to one for each dollar you must sign.

No IRS deductions will be taken out of your winnings. You are required to report these winnings to the IRS and believe me they have a record as I have seen the records.

If you win over five thousand to one on a ticket, the track will take a portion of your winnings and send it to the IRS for you. Isn't that nice?

Rarely would a win wager alone pay over three hundred to one so not to worry about win wagers. If you make a win wager of $20.00 and you horse wins at odds of forty to one you would collect $800.00 but no IRS form would be required because even though you won $800.00 the your ticket did not go over the three hundred to one part of the law. If you bet a $2.00 daily double or a $2.00 trifecta and the ticket paid over $600.00 on your $2.00 wager you will have to sign.

One way around not having to sign for every winner over three hundred to one or over $600.00 is to make your bets in one dollar amounts. Some tracks will not accept daily double wagers of less than $2.00 but virtually all tracks will accept all other exotic bets except the pick 6 for $1.00 amounts. If you win a $1.00 pick 3 and it pays $500. 00 for a dollar ticket you will not have to sign. If you play that same pick 3 ticket for $2.00 you would now win $1000.00 and have to sign. If you are playing exotic wagers and you feel there is any chance the ticket will pay over $600.00 then play it for a dollar and if you want to have two dollars on your wager then buy another ticket for another dollar. Any exotic wager than pays over the six hundred dollar limit will be a signer.

Another way around the rules applies to superfecta wagering. Buy your superfecta tickets in the ten cent amount. If you hit a superfecta and it pays $1000.00 for a dollar and you have a dollar on that ticket you will sign. If you buy the same superfeta for ten cents and but get it ten times you will get the same amount of money without a signature.

If you are playing via the computer your service provider will send you an IRS form each time you win over the IRS limit.

Consult your tax person about how to deduct your losses from winnings. Generally you can deduct losses only up the amount of your winnings.

Two last points about signers is that if you attempt to cash your ticket via the automated teller machines it will not work. The machine will tell you an IRS ticket can't be cashed at this machine. One last point to remember is that certain tracks will only cash your ticket if you have your Social Security card to show them. The Social Security administration tells you not to carry the card with you. One track which will remain unnamed would not cash my ticket until I came back with my card.

Final Comments

Now that we have discussed how to bet, when to bet, where to bet and what types of bets are available to make that small investment for large returns you are now ready to move on and give it a try.

Go slowly, play within the limits of your budget, and you will have some fun playing the horses. As you progress into the more sophisticated aspects of handicapping you will become more involved and learn to really love this game.

Always wait until that Official sign goes up before you start thinking about how much money you have just won. After the official, go collect your winnings but don't let everyone at the track know you are going to cash a big winning ticket. Anytime someone sees someone else with a lot of cash you become a potential target. Don't be afraid at the track but be discreet and be careful. People you don't know do not need to know you just won a lot of money.

If you find yourself getting involved on a routine basis and a couple of things start happening then take a few days off.

1. If you are losing every time you play or you have had a couple of winners taken down by the stewards
2. If you can't close your eyes without seeing horses running around a track take a break and if you are having dreams or can't sleep because of a bad few days at the track, then, for sure take a break for a few days until you are back in control.

Don't chase when you are behind. Don't start betting more than your comfort level allows. If you stay focused things will change. Slow down, take a deep breath and remember the concept that we started with at the beginning. Wager small amounts to win large amounts.

The challenge of picking winners is indeed not easy but when a horse you need to win is coming down the stretch and passing every other horse in his path the feeling you will have, will be one of exhilaration. It is not always about the money you are about to win, sometimes it is more about the fact that you figured out how the race was going to be run and you picked the winner. Enjoy the game, enjoy the people and it will become part of your life.

I had a friend who went to the track every day as it was his life. He didn't wager much but enjoyed the people and the racing game. He had a bugler hired prior to his death that came to the cemetery and played the … call to the post… for him, for the last time.

As virtually all race track announcers say just prior to a race. "It is now post time."

Made in United States
North Haven, CT
29 November 2023

44773305R00057